HIGHLIGHT REEL

Living Life Genuine, Blessed, and Fearless

By
Addie Lee Hention

Published by Victorious You Press™
Copyright © 2020 Addie Hention
All rights reserved.

No part of this book may be reproduced, distributed or transmitted in any form by any means, graphic, electronic, or mechanical, including photocopy, recording, taping, or by any information storage or retrieval system, without permission in writing from the author except in the case of reprints in the context of reviews, quotes, or references.

Unless otherwise indicated, scripture quotations are from the Holy Bible, King James Version. All rights reserved.

Printed in the United States of America

ISBN: 978-1-7340609-6-6

Special discounts are available on bulk quantity purchases by book clubs, associations, schools, churches etc. For details, email Addie Hention @reallifeexpressions1@gmail.com

Dedication

This book is dedicated to my Heavenly Father, who's first recorded words were – "Let there be light!" It is that light that has guided me along the best pathway for my life. Also, to the memory of my mother- Vivian Delores Prince and Sister-Christa Joy Larkins. Thank you for encouraging me to press on in my gift of writing before you passed on to heaven.

Acknowledgments

To my Husband – Michael Hention, thank you for being my restoration, my diamond in the rough, my number one fan, and best friend. I am so glad our paths crossed. You are proof that God is real!

To my Children – Tiara, Bryan, Makayla, and Gabriel. You all are the loves of my life and the jewels in my crown. I have been motivated to dream bigger and set better goals because of you.

To my cat – Starr, you keep a smile on my face with your precious presence.

To my Dad – Clyde Louis Prince, thank you for encouraging me to be the best I can be. I appreciate all your prayers and support.

To my Mom-in-Love, Ann Hention, I appreciate you for accepting and loving me. I admire the strong and virtuous woman that you are.

To my Sister & Brother in Love – Lorita & LeNoris Hightower, thank you for being the best sister and brother there is! Thank you and Jordan (my nephew) for being in my corner and keeping me in your prayers.

To my Fluellen Family – Thank you for being not just family but supporters of my dreams and goals.

To my Tribe – Kevin & Tracy; Darryl & Shelia Moreland, Terrance & Karla Jackson, Cousins Larry & Annabel, and Cousin Pat, words cannot express the blessings you are to Michael and me.

To Spiritual Leaders- K. Francis Smith of Excel Church; John and Terrie Elmore of 3D Church; and Michael Shreve of Mountain West, thank you for the spiritual mantles that you carry. Thank you for sharing God-given wisdom, life, and hope.

To my A-Team – Joan T. Randall of Victorious You Press, Angela McClain-Editor, Robyn Norwood-Editor, Eric & Maureen Quzack-Cover Designers, Will Brown, Jr. & Pallena Foreman of The Ark Studios, and The Millionaire Coach Consortium, thank you for your vision, positive critic and talents in collectively bringing this vision to pass.

To everyone who has dropped light and life into my life. You know who you are. Thank you!!

Contents

Introduction 1
Chapter 1: Lights, Camera, Action! 7
   Grand Entrance 7
   Just Following the Rules 11
   Ready for the World 16
Chapter 2: Deleted Scenes 21
   Take 5 22
   The Shame of It All 24
   Would Have, Should Have, Could Have 28
   Goodbye Failure! 32
Chapter 3: Musical Identity 35
   I Am 36
   The Meltdown 40
   Unlearning 43
   Becoming 46
Chapter 4: The Viewing Audience 49
   For the Love of Them 49
   The V.I.P. Section 51
   Saying "Goodbye" 54
   The Producer's Approval 55

Chapter 5: Chasing Waterfalls 59
A Field of Dreams 59
Reality Shock 62
More Equipped 64
Lessons Learned 66

Chapter 6: God's Plan 71
You Can't Go Back! 71
Losing My Way 74
Restored 76
Lessons Learned, Part 2 79

Chapter 7: To Be Real 81
Everyone Else Taken 82
Face to Face 85
Loving You 87
Being You 90

Chapter 8: Your Life Matters 95
Who Told You That?? 95
Worth Fighting For 99
Your Story, God's Glory 102

Chapter 9: Sincerely Yours 107
In the Beginning 107
Present Day 111
To Be Continued.... 113

About the Author 117

INTRODUCTION

When my husband and I moved into our housing subdivision, what stood out is how the houses do not look the same. Each home has its unique design of stucco or brick with or without wooden paneling.

The bedroom sizes can range from 3 to 6 bedrooms with 2 to 4 bathrooms. The landscaping of each house is manicured according to the Homeowners Association regulations and then according to the owner's unique taste. I think it is safe to say that the outside of each house is the owner's highlight reel. It is the curb appeal that catches one's eye. However, the real deal is what is going on behind closed doors.

Inside the home may be an immaculate living and dining area with a spacious kitchen and homey family room.

However, appearances can be deceiving. It is the human life and soul that makes its mark on the inside of a home. It is that living being who makes that house either a home or just a legal address.

You see, the things we choose to feature in life is our highlight reel. We have those aspects of our lives that are genuinely private and not for public display. Yet, there are other areas we may choose to hide or keep closed because of shame, embarrassment, or insecurity. There is no problem with the spotlight being shown on what has gone through a filter.

However, there is that part of you that goes out of the way to guard and protect what you do not want the spotlight on.

I started my conversation with you about a home because it is relatable. But, let us touch another area–Social Media. With the ability of different internet venues to communicate with family, friends, and people we do not know, we share our highlight reel. I have truly played my part in the "like, share, tag" campaign. I became a part of the Social Media world in June 2009. After a couple of friends encouraged me to share my inspirational thoughts and writings, I jumped on to motivate and inspire others.

I was labeled as a "thought leader," "an encourager," "a lifesaver," and "a rebel." To some, I tried to remain unique and authentic to the gift that stirred on the inside of me. However, after some time, I allowed myself to become a little compromised by highlighting what would bring cheers and likes.

Should the number of cheers and likes we do or do not receive make or break us? No. However, when it does matter, it is because we have lost sight of who we truly are and to whom we belong. One of my favorite Scripture passages is found in Psalm 139: 13-14 (NKJV). It reads as follows:

"For You formed my inward parts;

You covered me in my mother's womb.

I will praise You, for I am fearfully *and* wonderfully made;

Marvelous are Your works,

And *that* my soul knows very well."

Hmm... Selah (pause and think about it). You and I are fearfully and wonderfully made. No one, and I mean, NO ONE compares to you and me!

We are special, wonderful, beautiful, and worthy of the best God has for us! You might be saying, "Well, Ms. Addie, you do not know my story; and you do not know the things I have been through!"

You are right! I do not know your story or what you have been through; however, I do know that your life, your being here is not by accident or chance. Your highlight reel may not be as attractive as someone else's. Remember, a highlight reel is what people choose to put on display or allow you to see. It is their feature film. This does not mean that everything people share or put on display is fake. I want to make that clear. The point I am making is not to compete or compare with their highlight reel.

There is something we all want to have or improve upon in our lives. However, the driving force should be within our God-given purpose and wanting to maximize our fullest potential. When you know who you are and your purpose in life, you stop competing and comparing yourself with other people. In this book, I will be sharing principles and strategies to breaking free from an identity crisis, unrealistic expectations, guilt, shame, unworthiness, and the fear of living YOUR best life.

In this book, we will identify what currently forms our highlight reel. Together, we will walk through this journey of detoxing and renewing our minds. So, grab your favorite beverage and even feel free to grab a notepad and pen to jot down thoughts for your enrichment. As we travel through the pages of this book together, I will share personal stories, highs and lows, lessons learned, and wisdom gained from my life. I want us all to come to the end of this book with a better highlight reel. It is time to live a life that is genuine, blessed, and fearless! Let's do this!

Chapter 1:
LIGHTS, CAMERA, ACTION!

Grand Entrance

A star is born! The stage is set. It was a hot day, two days after the Fourth of July when I made my grand entrance into the world. I was introduced to my two young parents, who were filled with wonder and emotions upon having this little being. There was excitement in the family as I was the first grandchild to both of my grandmothers–Maggie and Frankie. Other loved ones welcomed me into the world. So, the spotlight is on me. Here I am breathing and existing outside of the safe place of my mother's womb. As all babies do, I eventually cry to communicate hunger, a poopy diaper, pain, or simply the need to be held. I had so much innocence and ignorance as I did not know the difference between right and wrong. I had yet to know the other intricate details of my existence such as my name, sex, social class, and ethnicity. There was so much to learn about this new world I was now living in.

The setting of the stage changes as I learn how to hold my bottle and eat solid food. I then learn how to sit up, crawl, pull up, walk, and eventually how to run. My parents begin to provide extra supervision as I discover and do crazy stuff like touching a socket. A swat is given on the back of my hand to let me know– "Addie, that is a no-no!" I grow up learning what is right and wrong through instruction, counsel, trial, and error. I begin to echo the melodies of my "ABC's" and counting to the number 10. I attended elementary school, middle school, and high school. I progressed through school and graduated from high school with pride. I am a star amongst other stars who made it to one of the most important days of their lives. I stood on the stage of my high school production facing the unknown of adulthood. I was naïve to the experiences awaiting me beyond the 12 years of education I had received.

Turning 18 years of age in July, I thought I was grown. Well, not really. I was old enough to vote, participate in Jury Duty, drive with a valid driver's license, and enlist in the Armed Forces, but I was still immature and, in some cases, premature. People told me that turning 21 years old is when I would be a real grown-up. At this age, you can buy alcohol, cigarettes, and gamble. I did none of these things, but there was a glide in my stride in knowing that I could if I wanted to. There I was wanting to move forward with underdeveloped wisdom and without knowing my true purpose in life. However, I still considered myself to be a star pursuing a leading role in life. Can you relate to this picture I am painting?

I started by saying, "A star is born" because it is true. A star is what we all are. God once spoke to a man named Abraham and told him to look up and count the stars. However, there were and presently are too many stars to count. Each Star has light and twinkles to a special rhythm. At the beginning of our existence is a purpose and potential that so many of us do not realize we have. We are given a name that we begin to answer to after being called upon repeatedly. And, let us not mention the nicknames given to us like Peanut, Boo-Boo, Sweet Pea, Stinky, or Junior just to name a few. When I think about it, where do we come up with these crazy nicknames for our children? Some are terms of endearment. While others may describe how people see us as a child. Some descriptions can leave a stigma that can be challenging to shake off as the years go by.

Speaking of names and labeling, I once named myself "Peaches" when I was in middle school because I thought it was cool. When T-shirts were made for my eighth-grade class, I was sure to have that name engraved on the back of my shirt. However, I recall the hurt of being called "slow." I was considered slow in alethic ability and slow in academics. I overcame my academic challenges, but a stigma was left in athletics for years, because of the word "slow." As a young adult, I would not participate in group sports. I would do well in playing one on one at playing sports like volleyball or badminton. But when others wanted to join in, I would quickly excuse myself. I was afraid of being talked about when the activities simply existed out of pure fellowship and fun. If I only knew how much God loved me and had a plan for my life.

Just Following the Rules

In my childhood, I wanted to please my parents, I wanted my teachers to see me as a star student, and I wanted other family and church folks to say that I was a good kid. Yes, I was a good kid for the most part. I tried to uphold the rules given to me. However, I did have my moments of being sneaky and breaking a few rules behind the scenes. As with any young person, I had to learn the meaning of honor and integrity and doing what was right because it was right not simply out of following the rules. I grew up in a religious home with strictness and dared not clown my parents too much. There were consequences like going to our room and waiting for a spanking, being dismissed from the dinner table, no TV, and special privileges removed. My home was the first place among other places of learning to do what I was told.

Another place of following the rules was at school. I know many of you are familiar with the drills and routines that are given to us as children while attending school. At school, you must be on time or get marked tardy. If you are absent from school, you must have a signed excuse from your parent or guardian. You must do your homework and turn it back in on time. During the school day, you must line up in a single file to go to the bathroom or lunch. When you wanted to speak or be heard, you had to raise your hand first. I was quiet and nerdy, and I did not fit in with my peers. My focus was on being in the good graces of my teachers. Despite this goal, I still had a few teachers who were not fond of me for whatever reason. A gym coach in elementary school sided with students in making fun of my poor athletic ability. This led to my being in a shell when it came to team sports. Elementary school and middle school were not good parts of my highlight reel, but those years played a part in shaping and molding my story.

Before we go any further, I must mention the religious part of my life. As mentioned earlier, I grew up in a religious home. The requirements for honoring God in my home were to attend Sunday School and worship service. There were times when going to church was an all-day thing. Ladies were required to wear a dress, tights, or stockings with neat hair. The gentlemen were required to enter the House of God with suits or at the very least, a shirt and tie with neatly pressed pants and dress shoes. In my household, I grew up "Pento-Baptist." This means I grew up both Pentecostal and Baptist. The Lord was represented differently in both religious genres. However, I learned to follow and uphold the rules of both denominations. You learned when you should stand, sit, say "Amen" and "Hallelujah," and shout. After all, following the rules meant pleasing God, right?

Please! Do not get me wrong; I am not anti-church. I respect rules and the need for order.

I love church fellowship, but I love God much more. I say this in light of coming to know God for myself, not religion or a bunch of rules. While we are on the subject, I did not realize how much I had integrated religion into the lives of my children. I wanted them to look and dress the part to please God until an awakening took place in me. In my efforts to give my children Jesus, I passed on what I thought was right at that time. I began to shift my focus from religion to a relationship with God and knowing Him for myself. I had to learn to separate God from the flaws and shortcomings I saw in some people who misrepresented Him. Also, my focus began to shift more on a person's character than titles and years in "God's service."

Another place of following the rules is in the workplace. My first job was in the fast-food industry. I started on the cash register and then the drive-through. I was excited about getting my feet wet to work and earning my first paycheck. I soon learned that I had to be on time and call ahead if I would be out or running late. As a cashier, I had to receive and return the correct amount of money. There was a checklist of duties to follow during your shift. The checklist involved smiling at customers and greeting them properly, restocking condiments and paper items, wiping down tables, etc. I remember the one time I was given a warning and wrote up for having a short drawer. I was devasted. I aimed to pay more attention to detail moving forward. In this work scenario, I learned to do what pleased others to uphold the rules and keep my job.

Again, rules and regulations are important, provided they are in good taste and within ethics. Rules provide boundaries and standards. However, the downside is becoming a "yes person" and doing what pleases people at the expense of compromising what makes you authentic. I briefly reflect on situations where I truly believed I was pleasing God and doing the right thing, only to realize I was not being true to myself. I was aiming to "please" in situations that God had nothing to do with. I had to learn to be more discerning and use common sense where it applied. I also had to learn that going along just to get along was not always the best thing to do. Does this lesson resonate with anyone else?

Ready for the World

I want to take you back to the set of my high school senior year. I was ready to face the world with naivety and lacked knowledge of what it truly meant to be an adult. After I graduated from Murray-Wright High School in Detroit, I remember proclaiming to my mom that I was grown now. My parents slowly began to remove their support allowing me to see for myself that being "grown" was not as easy as it looked. I soon realized that being grown was more than just being of legal age, having voting rights, going to jury duty, attending a university, getting a job, and making my own choices after turning 21 years of age. School taught me discipline and structure for daily living along with reading, writing, arithmetic, and college prep. However, I soon came to realize that LIFE came with many tests and lessons that a diploma or college degree could never give me. In school, you learn the lessons then take the tests, but in life, you take the tests and learn the lessons.

At the age of 19, I found myself at a place that was very uncomfortable and lacking direction. A fallout with my parents led to me being in a place of uncertainty. I temporarily found shelter in the home of a beloved friend I had met in middle school and her family. I stayed with them while attending college and working a part-time job at Hardee's. This home was filled with love and God. However, Mama B did not play. I had to respect the rules of the house and be honest about my travels. I learned that being a young adult came with dangers and responsibilities. More importantly, I learned that freedom was not free. During this delicate season of growth, my spirituality went to a different level. I stepped away from what was a tradition to following a path of getting closer to God.

My folks thought I was crazy for choosing a nondenominational place of worship, but I needed to connect with God in a way that became personal and real to me. I had my ups and downs, got heartbroken, and had to begin the long process of character development. My attempts at doing what was right would be met by occasional failure along with hits and misses.

Through the years, I have found strength in the following scripture in Psalm 37:23-24, which says-

> *"The steps of a good man are ordered by the LORD,*
> *And He delights in his way.*
> *Though he falls, he shall not be utterly cast down;*
> *For the LORD upholds him with His hand."*

This Scripture reminded me that I was loved and someone greater was keeping me. I was a young adult searching for purpose and meaning. I was learning to overcome my hurt and pain. In the process, I would hurt others and inflict pain on myself, which I will get into in another chapter. My highlight reel has had its moments of triumph and failures. Yet, this is all a part of living, learning, and growing. I have learned not to allow fear, guilt, and shame to dominate my life. My friend, I want to encourage you to do the same. Now, I know this is easier said than done, but as you keep walking with me on this journey, I pray your burdens will be lifted as you learn to let go and let God.

Being ready for the world means to have faith and trust in someone greater than you. You draw on the power that resides on the inside of you. You must know that God has you no matter what life challenges you with. No matter what you have been through or come from, your life is not void of purpose. The good, the bad, and ugly can work out for your good!

Chapter 2:
DELETED SCENES

"Failure is not final."

To keep it "100" with you, I have struggled in sharing certain parts of my story with you. While doing housework one day, the Lord spoke to my heart and encouraged me not to be pretty in sharing my story, but to share from my heart. I am sharing things in this chapter, not for the sake of drawing attention to myself or drawing sympathy. I share from my heart to help someone to break free of the fear, guilt, and shame that tries to keep you bound. Those scenes that are cut or hidden from our life story contribute to the essence of our being. We tuck these scenes in the archives of our life, but facing them sets us free and empowers us to help others. Let us move forward in this highlight reel process with a special discussion on deleted scenes.

Take 5

In the workplace and the film industry, you "take 5" to break from production. Here, we will talk about the breaks we take from life and the do-overs to make things better. After all, we want to have a highlight reel, a feature film that is impressive, right? Take a walk with me on my career path. Like most people, on this pathway, I was trying to find significance and purpose. As a young child, I wanted to be a schoolteacher and would play school with my dolls and stuffed animals. Then, I wanted to be a nurse. For a moment, I saw myself as a story writer. I developed a love for reading and writing. However, I settled on a career in business. I started with Computer Science as a major, but that was short-lived as I realized that numbers and writing programs did not fit my profile. The switch was made to Records Management. This was it! Well, at least for a moment. My pursuit of higher education was interrupted by my need for love. Yes, I had love on my mind!

This guy was a familiar face with a voice I loved to hear over the phone. Cell phones were not the highlight of communication just yet. So, holding the house phone up to your ear and even falling asleep while on the phone was a thing at the time. I remember family and friends getting annoyed when you held up the telephone to indulge in your conversation. Now, back to my love interest. I met this guy before starting college. Two years went by as he had left to be in the military. He was back on military leave and wanted to reconnect. However, little did I know that his "leave" was the result of a dishonorable discharge. He was back in town to find a job and make ends meet. Now, my silly tail lacked discernment, and I did not ask the right questions. I found myself in a relationship with a young man, who sold drugs for a living. He reported to a drug dealer. As a result, being in his company was risking business. How could I have let this happen? I ended up at odds with my folks and temporarily dropped out of college. When I foresaw a future with him that was less than God's best, I woke up. I walked away from the relationship in one piece.

After almost a year on hiatus, I was back in school, continuing what I started. I still wanted love in my life, but I kept myself grounded enough to receive my Bachelor's in Business Administration. It took me six years, but I finished. During employment with a bank in Detroit, I received a promotion after nine months of working in the Wire Transfer Department. I felt proud and blessed as I was on my way as a young professional. However, I kept self-sabotaging myself. I was following a plan of success by my standards, but I kept running into the same wall of mental instability and looking for love in the wrong faces and places. I needed a wakeup call in knowing God's purpose for my life, and His endless love for me and having a healthy love for myself.

The Shame of It All

I lived in Mississippi for a season. While attending a church service one Sunday morning, a young woman walked up to me and said, "No more fear. No more guilt. No more shame." I knew I was carrying unhealthy things, but the baggage was heavier than I wanted to admit. I was weighed down with things that I needed to be set free from. The mask and costume of spirituality and religion kept me out of plain sight of the obvious. For someone else, their mask and costume might be a career, job title, or social-economic status. You can be gifted, anointed, appointed, and good at what you do. Yet, you are still in need of deliverance. Upon receiving that word from the sister at church, I was at a low point. I was at a place of rethinking decisions and why I had ended up in my present predicament.

Time travel with me for a moment. As mentioned in the intro of this chapter, there are scenes you would like to delete altogether from your life. For me, it was a moment in time when I felt helpless as I felt like a science experiment on an examination table at a children's medical center. Where was my Mom? Who were these people? Why are these pictures being taken? I was told the pictures were for medical purposes. I was not sexually abused, and no pictures were taken of my private parts, but I felt violated. I never spoke up about how I felt. I felt as if my speaking up would not be heard as I was still elementary school age. I lived with this shame for years. I thank God for keeping my mind and keeping my destiny protected despite this scar. I went through my life fighting with demons and being half crazy. I suffered in silence with this hurt and pain for years. I suppressed a situation that haunted the crap out of me. Facing and releasing it has brought freedom.

There have been other moments like when my drug-dealing boyfriend grabbed me by the neck during an intense argument. We were arguing about something and our tempers flared. In a fit of rage, he backed me into a wall and grabbed me by the neck. However, out of nowhere, he suddenly let me go and turned to walk outside. It was if he had seen a ghost. God's presence intervened. I also know that somebody somewhere was praying for me. So many moments were all but for the grace of God! I do not know what you have been through in your life that has brought shame along with guilt and fear. Whatever it was that you have chosen to cut from your highlight reel, I hope this Scripture in Isaiah 54 brings you comfort as it did for me. Verse 4 reads as follows:

> *"Do not fear, for you will not be ashamed;*
> *Neither be disgraced, for you will not be put to shame;*
> *For you will forget the shame of your youth,*
> *And will not remember the reproach of your widowhood anymore."*

This Scripture does not mean that all your memories of the past will be erased. This is quite the contrary. If this is the case, why do we study history in school? We make a record of historical accounts to review events and why they occurred. We look at a person's part in history and the impact their decisions had on our society. Everyone's story comes with a history, either good or bad. This Bible Scripture is letting us know that once we surrender the fear, guilt, and shame of our past over to God, those things no longer have power over us. We can no longer be held captive by things that made us feel powerless or that we cannot change.

Would Have, Should Have, Could Have

We have plants in our front yard that give the outside of our home a nice touch. One day, while coming into our home, I noticed a strange plant growing alongside the nice ones. When our lawn guy made another trip by the house, he identified them as weeds and cut them out. Would have, should have, and could have are all rooted in regret. Regret is a weed that must be uprooted and cut from our lives. Are there things I wish I could have done differently? Yes! I will not lie to you on this fact. If I could time travel, a lot of adjustments would be made. However, in light of something significant being altered, it is best to let the past be the past.

During a visit to Mississippi in 2017 for my oldest daughter's graduation from Mississippi State University, a group of us stopped at a Chick-Fil-A for a quick bite to eat. Out of quick thought and curiosity, I began to ask each family member, "If you could go back in time, what time in history would you visit? Who would you like to meet?" When I got around to my son, he said- "No one." So, I asked him why? He replied, "Because, one little change could throw off the present." This made me think about the alterations I would end up making to my present and future that might not turn out as well as expected.

Think for a moment about what you could change or do better if you could. To be honest and knowing what I know now, there are men I would not have dated and decisions I would not have made. Also, there are setbacks I would have avoided. My mature and wiser self would go back in time and have a nice discussion with my younger self. However, I cannot go back, and neither can you. What you and I can do is learn from the setbacks, failures, and mistakes. If something happened that was beyond your control, thank God you came through the situation in your right mind, in one piece, and with a testimony to share with others. Somethings we go through in life are a part of our process for growth and development. There is no testimony without tests. There is no message without a mess. Check out this Scripture passage with me in Romans 8:28.

"And we know that all things work together for good to those who love God, to those who are called according to His purpose."

The Scripture passage we just looked at together usually gets misquoted. People will quote the first part and leave out the second part, which is equally important. The word "purpose" cannot be ignored. Your divine purpose and destiny bring beauty, light, and life when God is writing and editing your story. There is no pain without purpose. There is no process without purpose. I used to sit up, cry, and ridicule myself over dumb decisions and situations I wished were done differently. I did not realize I was indulging in self-hatred. To keep mulling over things you cannot change is like crying over spilled milk. You cannot pick up the milk and put it back in the glass. The option is to clean up the mess, start over, and keep it moving.

On occasion, I and my husband will go through the special features on a DVD and review the deleted scenes section. We get a chance to see how a scene would have added to or taken away from the flow of the final edit to a film. As we continue in this highlight reel experience, I want to encourage someone to not be ashamed of what you have been through. Thank God you made it through! Do not keep reminiscing over what could have been done better. When you know better, do better. Each day is a new start. You start over again! Share the wisdom gained and lessons learned with others. Your story is for God's glory!

Goodbye Failure!

Goodbye failure! It's over between you and me.

I will no longer allow you to tell me who I am not or what I cannot be.

Every time I settled for average, you grinned and folded your arms in satisfaction.

I am reaching for the stars and will live life without fear or intimidation.

I am strong enough to realize there are things I cannot change.

I forgive myself, forgive others, and I refuse to remain the same.

You keep telling me that I cannot make it without you.

However, it seems that you need me way more than I need you.

I will no longer allow you to drain me of strength and suck the life out of me.

I know who I am and will boldly pursue all I was meant to be.

No more cloudy days or moods of blue.

I will grow from the lessons, but I don't need you.

Laugh if you wish and tell me I need to stop dreaming.

But, through the eyes of faith, I see myself winning.

Your reign is over, and there's the door.

I see a new beginning and will sorrow no more.

Goodbye failure!

By: Addie Lee Hention

Chapter 3:
MUSICAL IDENTITY

"God can only bless who you truly are, not who you pretend to be."

-Michael Todd

How often do you meet a new you? Stay with me, because I am going somewhere with this. It is known as a myth to some, but it is scientifically proven by those who study human behavior that our bodies and minds change every seven years. Interesting, huh? I have taken notes of my growing process and pains over the years. I am not just referring to the physical changes in height, weight, foot size, the need for eyeglasses, etc. I am also referring to the spiritual, mental, and emotional changes that take place in response to an environment, situation, and people. There have been changes in fashion, the coloring of hair, the disgust of certain foods, the acquired taste of coffee, and the search to know God in a real way. Let us delve into the highlight reel of identity.

I Am

"I Am" usually begins in our childhood. My parents named me Addie, which means "noble." My parents named me after my Great-Grandmother on my father's side. I understand my dad had a great love and admiration for her. I remember learning to write my first name "Addie" repeatedly until I knew how to spell it. Then came the practice of learning my last name, which at the time was "Prince." So, when someone would ask me what my name was, the response was "Addie." Other inquiring formalities followed, such as "How old are you?" "What school do you attend?" "What grade are you in?" Let us not leave out the ethnic label. I had to identify myself as black. I would look in the mirror and look at my skin, and think to myself, "I am not black! I am brown!" Eventually, this ethnic label became known as African American. Of course, there were other classifications such as gender, birthplace, social-economic status, and religion. If you are like me, it took some time to realize there is more to you than these labels and classifications.

Being told who you are and getting to the place of knowing who you are without insecurity or reservation takes time. This is especially true if you had to fight through negative labeling as some do in childhood and even as adults. As a child, being told that you are loved without any hidden agendas is one of the greatest things in shaping our persona and character. However, it is very destructive to be told things like "You are ugly." You are stupid." "You are slow." "You will never amount to anything." Think for a moment of how it feels to even hear those statements. You do not want to start your day off declaring those things over your life. One of the most hurtful things I had to overcome was being called "slow." As a young student, I struggled through elementary and part of middle school academically. The label of "slow" did not help my progress, not to mention being bullied.

My mom was impatient and frustrated with my learning ability. I could not grasp certain concepts and principles until a light bulb came on. Thank God for someone praying for me and School House Rock.

Growing up in a religious household, I took solace in the first Bible given to me. It was a Children's Living Bible with pictures. I would read the stories in Genesis of characters like Adam & Eve, Joseph with the Coat of Many Colors, and Moses. I would read and learn the 23rd Psalm and The Beatitudes. I attended church regularly with my mom and dad. When they chose to attend different churches from one another, I alternated my church attendance between the two of them. I learned religious protocols for both the Church of God in Christ and the Baptist church. I soon developed a deeper hunger for God and faith on my own. I was God's child, a chosen vessel, and new creation in Christ. Yet, I kept having a struggle within, between light and darkness. The "new me" kept fighting with the "old me." I had to learn this fight will never cease and the importance of feeding my spirit and soul with light and life.

Before we close out this segment, there is the "I Am" associated with being someone's "boo," "honey," "significant other," or "spouse." The relationship can be solid or complicated. I remember taking great pride in being a man's "woman" or "girl" until the relationship went south. I had my fair share of crushes, infatuations, romances, and heartbreaks before being married to my wonderful husband, Michael. The "I Am" had to be redefined when I was no longer kicking it or coupled with someone. I did not cease to be me because the relationship ended. I was still Addie. However, I had to realize that I never knew who I was apart from the relationship. Does this sound familiar to you or remind you of a situation involving someone you know? I had to find the real me, cultivate, and water my spirit and soul according to God's design and plan.

Let me recap a few things I have shared in this segment of "I Am." We have our name, race, ethnicity, gender, social-economics, and what people call us. These labels and classifications establish a foundation for who we will become. So, considering where your journey is taking you, ask yourself, "Who am I?".

The Meltdown

Wow! This part right here is deep for me. After turning 40 years old, I came to an abrupt place in my life that led me to a fork in the road. To be more candid, my 40's were rough. Society talks about the midlife crisis. Well, I guess I had my dose of it. My mental and emotional health was challenged. I was at a place where I realized that some of the things that once brought me security and strength could not suffice me anymore. Here I was divorced, a single parent, living in Mississippi, with hopes and dreams crumbling. I still had my faith and trust in God. But, my faith and trust in God were challenged in the face of the crossroads I was standing in. I was confronted with the realization that my "highlight reel" was not authentic and genuine. My identity had been attached to things that did not allow me to be the rare diamond I was meant to be.

I had been proud of the accomplishments I made in the face of adversity. Yet, I found myself feeling empty and spiritually dislocated. Should I have been focusing more on my achievements and less on what was not happening in my life? Yes. However, I needed to confront this giant of mistaken identity to genuinely move forward. As a single mom, I felt like I should have been in a place of being able to give my children more. Yet, I found comfort in knowing that God was with us and always provided. I had to fight off feelings of inadequacy from no longer being married. I felt like I was nothing without a man. It is amazing how much of our identity can be tied up in a person, place, or thing. I could no longer say, "I am Mrs...." I had to realize that I was still Addie. I had to migrate from being divorced to being "single-again." The term "single-again" sounded much better than being "divorced." The realization hit me that I had much to learn about what it meant to truly be single. I will say more on this subject for another book and time.

My career path had been on a roller coaster of highs and lows. Like most teenagers and young adults, I started off working in the restaurant business. At the time, it was no big deal, because I was proud to be working. After two years of working in restaurants, I made the following declaration: "This will be my last year working in a restaurant!" I applied for office jobs and ended up being hired in the Wire Transfer Department of a bank in Detroit. During my first year on this job, I completed my college education. It was a blessing to no longer say- "I am a cashier. "I am a waitress." or "I am a hostess." Do not get me wrong, there is nothing wrong with working in restaurants. I made up my mind that I wanted better for myself. Back then, I did not realize the power of my words. I have not worked in a restaurant since.

Since entering the workforce, I worked many jobs for several businesses. If "I am" had remained attached to any of those jobs, I would be lost. When a season ended with a company, I had to learn that I was still Addie. Everywhere I went "I" would be right there. The same is true for you. As you navigate through life, your positions and assignments may change, but you are still (say your name). To take it a step further, you are still a Child of God. You are still loved. You are still destined for greatness. You are still valued. You are still worthy. You are favored by God. You have a purpose. When we do not know who we truly are, we go on an endless search to find ourselves and the true meaning of life through relationships, places, and things. It can put you in a place of developing a mindset and habits that are not good and need to be changed.

Unlearning

I accomplished twelve years of schooling in K-5 through 12th grade, six years of college, two years of Bible school along with years of special training only to realize I still had much to learn. During school, you learn the lessons, practice through homework, and then take a test to get a passing grade. However, in life, you take tests and then you learn the lessons. What I just said does not seem right, but it seems to be the way life goes in general. There is always something new to learn. There is a takeaway from any situation. I have found that lessons turn into blessings when you gain wisdom, knowledge, and understanding. However, the real challenge for me has been with the things I have had to unlearn.

What we know or think we know can be so embedded in us to the point where we become set in our ways. Habits and routines come with branding that says, "This is just the way I am." However, having always been a certain way does not mean you have to stay that way. Just because something has always been done a certain way, does not mean it cannot be improved upon. A quote from the Serenity Prayer by Reinhold Niebuhr says,

> *"God grant me the serenity to accept the things I cannot change, courage to change the things I can, and wisdom to know the difference."*

Some things will always remain solid to me like my relationship with God, faith, marriage, family, peace, health, and productive work. To be completely honest with you, what I have had to learn and unlearn has affected every area of my life. I had to unlearn self-hatred and learn to love myself as God sees me. I have not always been my own best friend. I struggled with my identity like someone trying to get in and out of clothes that do not fit your body and shape well. As a result, I would attract some people into my life who fed my dysfunction. What was toxic in me attracted the same in others. These relationships seemed normal until I realized the need for better associates and acquaintances in my life. The process of loving myself and not giving up on myself began upon realizing how much God loved me. "We love because He first loved us." (I John 4:19).

Another process I had to go through was unlearning religion and learning to know God for myself. Church had its place in connecting me to God and teaching basic Bible principals living. I am grateful for that. However, the church taught me how to be religious, self-righteous, traditional, and to play dress up. I mean no disrespect in what I just said, but it is the highlight reel I once lived in. I used to think that being in church every Sunday and Mid-Week Bible Study was the ticket to Heaven. However, all God wanted and all I needed was a genuine heart-to-heart relationship with Him. I needed to know God's love for me was not based on performance or being connected to a certain religious affiliation. He loved me as I was, the way I was and would help me to become all the woman I was meant to be. Ephesians 2:8 says,

> *"For by grace you have been saved through faith, and that not of yourselves; it is the gift of God, not of works lest any man should boast."*

My salvation was not through works, but through grace by faith. I wished I had come into this realization sooner in life, but it is better late than never.

Becoming

Once upon a time, there was a little girl who was shy, insecure, curious, and sneaky. While this is an interesting description to give myself as a little girl, this is where my highlight reel was at that time in my life. Many times, I would run home as I was picked on and bullied by a few kids at the school. I was told not to get into fights, which resulted in me feeling alone. Being the oldest of three siblings, I had to learn to stand up for myself. As time went on, the views others had of me were nerdy, a bookworm, quiet, sneaky, and an Oreo (black on the outside, but white in the middle). I loved to read, research, and listen to a mixture of music. I eventually stepped into full effect with hairstyles and outfits representing the season I was living in. I once spent a lot of time on my hair and would change the color of it often. I was growing, developing, learning, experimenting, and facing truths that sometimes hurt.

I once felt that hitting certain milestones like finishing college, taking my first plane trip, getting married, having children, and turning 30 made me a woman, but this was not true. I hit milestones without connecting myself to the purpose and plan God had for my life. As I am sharing with you, I realized that I was just checking things off my list without having a strong "why" for what I was doing. I had to learn that the decisions we make affect more than just yourself. Some decisions, good or bad, can have a ripple effect on our future and those connected to us.

My womanhood came into being through gaining wisdom, knowledge, and understanding through the lessons of life. My "becoming" involved maturity, responsibility for choices made, and reclaiming my genuine identity. As we close out this chapter together, I want to ask you the following questions:

"Who have you become?"

"Are you satisfied with where you are?"

"What makes your life complete?"

In answering these questions, I hope you were honest with yourself? Being real when faced with these types of questions leads to wholeness. If you are good with where you are and only need to fine-tune, that is wonderful. If you feel you are a hot mess, do not despair. Truth be told we all are a work in progress. Again, the key element is being honest with yourself, and work on becoming the man or woman God has designed you to be.

Chapter 4:
THE VIEWING AUDIENCE

"If I live before the audience of One before others, I have nothing to gain, nothing to prove, and nothing to lose."

-O.S. Guinness

For the Love of Them

As I share with you in this segment, words from an old school jam are ringing in my heart. It is "For the Love of You" by the Isley Brothers. If the Lord does not speak to me through a Gospel song, there are times when songs from other genres will do the job of driving a point home. The lyrics in this song by this legendary R&B

group fits the subject matter. The love that we give and receive can be either healthy or dysfunctional. I say this because I have been on both sides of the fence where love is concerned. The giving and receiving of love can be a complex thing. It involves wanting to be accepted or validated. You want the viewing audience to always leave positive reviews about you, or to leave a rating of "excellent" or "very good" on a five-point scale. When you do not get the love and approval you want, it can leave you with questions about your value and worth.

Even though I knew God loved this dark child, I did not understand the value and worth I already had. A great man of God once said, "When you do not know the value of a thing, you will abuse it." There I was, not once but several times, lowering and compromising myself to be loved and accepted. A stamp of approval was something I needed to feel validated. I found myself living for the love of my folks, a man, coworkers, and some saints. Being a blessing and helping where needed is a good thing. However, making small compromises to get approval is another story. One thing I had to learn is when people genuinely love you, you do not have to be someone you are not. You do not have to sell your soul for approval or acceptance. The love you give and the love you receive is to be rooted in God. We will now move on to discuss some important people–The VIP section of the viewing audience.

The V.I.P. Section

The meaning of the acronym for V.I.P. is a "very important person." I want you to think with me for a moment of what a "V.I.P." means to you personally if not professionally. Several years ago, I found out about a group of Gospel singers coming to town. It turned out that they would be performing a free concert to benefit a special cause. However, if you wanted to be in the front section, you had to purchase V.I.P. tickets. If my memory serves me correctly, I paid $15 each for myself and two children. I was a single parent at the time and cherished any moment that was a break from our daily hustle and bustle. Anyway, my purchase of those V.I.P. tickets landed us in the second row. It was awesome to see Carman, Fred Hammond, Crystal Lewis, and other singers up close. We were very important people for that evening because of where we were sitting. In our personal lives, who do we allow or choose to have in our V.I.P. section?

Our highlight reel includes these very important people. For me, the people who automatically had the front row in my life for many years were my mother, father, and sisters. When there was a special occasion like a concert, play, award ceremony or graduation, it meant the world to me to see them present. It was a bonus to see other people present for special moments in my life like a grandparent, uncle, aunt, cousin, or family friend. However, in passing years, many people have come and gone due to either passing away, relocating, opposing views, or change in seasons. As I am sharing with you, I am briefly reflecting on how people come into your life for a reason and a season. I have had to learn that not everyone is with you for a lifetime. Few people are with you through winter, spring, summer, and fall. Proverbs 17:17 says, *"A friend loves at all times, and a brother is born for adversity."* It is important to have people in your life who are there through sunshine and rain, and joy and pain. We would refer to these people as ride or die.

I used to be loose with deeming someone as a friend. As an adult, I found myself dealing with the harsh reality that everyone is not your friend. As a result, I made sure my children received wisdom on friendships. We must discern why a person is present and what the purpose of the connection is. The purpose of a person's presence in your life and you in theirs has a deeper significance when it is connected to God's plan. I call these relationships "divine connections." Your steps are ordered by God to meet the right person, at the right place, and at the right time. I thank God for the human angels who have come into my life over the years. I thank God for those whose presence served as a blessing and a lesson. When people leave the V.I.P. section of your life willingly or because they cannot go where God is taking you, it can hurt. However, let me say this, some people move on because they have fulfilled their season in your life. You must trust and surrender those relationships to God.

Saying "Goodbye"

Let me be the first to say that I hate goodbyes. Goodbye can be bitter-sweet and associated with hurt and pain of separation from a person, place, or thing. To this very moment, I miss my grandmother, mom, and sister, who have gone on to Heaven before me. I also miss other beloved relatives and solid relationships I once had. These people are no longer apart of the physical viewing audience of my life because their time on Earth is no more. There are people in our lives who are alive and well, but their part in your story has been served. In June of 2002, I moved away from Detroit, Michigan with my two young children to Jackson, Mississippi. I cried as a drove off into the unknown with the valuables we had on the Budget Rental truck. The reason for this move was that I had taken a job with a satellite church that was an offspring to the headquarters ministry in Michigan. At times, I ponder the investment of that move as it came with unexpected challenges. Yet, there were miracles and special moments that were truly a God thing. I said, "goodbye" to pursue what I believed to be a calling from God.

On the other hand, "goodbye" is for the best when a person, place, or thing is defeating your destiny, originality, and purpose. Think with me for a moment of who and what you had to say "goodbye" to because it was for the best. Saying "goodbye" can be difficult even when it needs to be done. This process was difficult because I did not want to come off as a villain or a bad person. Also, I would think about the investment I made, and time spent only to give that situation "the left hand of fellowship." I had to have the courage to show that person or thing the exit sign. If you are holding on to something or someone hoping that things will change, pray, and ask God to help you do what is best. As I mentioned a little earlier in this chapter, trust and surrender those relationships and situations to God.

The Producer's Approval

A few years back, I quoted the following on Facebook, "In order to be a blessing to people, you must get free from people." Trying to please everyone and keep them happy is a violation of your peace. It is impossible to please and keep everyone happy. Whenever I am on YouTube, I cannot help but notice no matter what video is posted, no matter how good I think a song or conversation is, there is always someone giving it a "dislike." When you are on Facebook or Twitter, you may post something only to get a few likes. What do you do? Do you leave the post up or take it down based on the lack of responses you received? I will admit to removing posts throughout my years on Social Media because I did not get the feedback I wanted. I had to learn that whatever I shared was not for everybody. I had to stop posting based on what I thought would please everybody. The posts I share and the post that you share should be what is true and genuine.

There are people directly involved in our lives who may not get us or understand our purpose. As a result, it can be disheartening when some people that we value the most do not approve of what we are doing. Personally, it would hurt when a family member, friend or spiritual leader criticized or gave a thumbs down to something or someone important to me. Because of the position these VIP's held in my life, their approval meant the world to me. However, I had to learn as a grown adult and walking my path that every decision I made was not going to receive five stars. I also had to learn that just because someone did not agree with me, it does not mean they are against me. We just do not see eye to eye. Now, I am not talking about rejecting wise counsel. However, if what was on my heart to pursue was based on following God and a solid vision, I had to rest in knowing I was doing the right thing and keep moving forward.

My story and your story are timeless classics. Everyone's journey is unique and is to be valued and respected by others. We must watch the amount of control we give to people just because we want their approval. Our Heavenly is the producer of personal stories and scripts that are given to us. In Him, we live, move, and have our being (Acts 17:28). While having people in our corner is important, we should not live for approval or be easily discouraged by the lack of it. We are to live for an audience of one. God is the higher power that I look to for strength, wisdom, and direction. Each day is a fresh page to make the most of this life given to us. You and I can no longer waste time on having a highlight reel with bells and whistles that are not authentic to who we truly are. He wants us to walk through each season of our lives with grace and dignity. While we cannot change things from the past or control everything that crosses our path, we know that there is a power within us to withstand adversity. That same power will help us to keep dreaming, believing, and walking by faith. The producer of our lives has plans that are for our good and not evil (Jeremiah 29:11). God will take anything that is meant to throw us off-script and turn it around for our good.

Chapter 5:
CHASING WATERFALLS

"Sometimes you win and sometimes you learn."

-Breeny Lee

A Field of Dreams

Do these two scenarios sound familiar to you? She is a beautiful princess waiting for her knight and shining armor. He is a superhero–a mighty warrior and defender of the universe. The imagination that a child has can be endless. As a child, I believed I could do and become anything I imagined. I would sometimes use my imagination to escape from the reality of falling short academically and being teased in school. It was my safe place. I was barely 12 years old and began writing a little drama series about an imaginary family in my notebook. Oh, and I was also a hopeless romantic at a young age in terms of my dreams and imagination. I would put myself in the shoes of certain characters from cartoons or human movies that were rated "G" or "PG" rated. As time went on, I learned to lean towards more realistic dreams and squash the fantasies.

I chased after what I thought to be "living the dream" like having a college degree, a good job, marriage, and family. I want to be clear in saying there is nothing wrong with the things I just mentioned. However, I was lacking purpose along with a strong "Why?" I would dare to say that most of us did not focus on the purpose of a thing or why we wanted to have it. For me, "purpose" and "why" is something I had to learn to apply after a series of hurt and failure. I would see how beautiful a thing was in hindsight without realizing the responsibility or danger that came with it. I was chasing waterfalls. In all honesty, while accomplishing some goals, I chased after waterfalls for a long time. I was determined to have a highlight reel that my parents and others would be proud of.

After my first marriage ended in divorce, I found myself starting over again, I got involved with serving in the church I was a member of at that time. Eventually, I felt pulled towards Bible School and followed that path. The process of Bible School along with raising two young children and working part-time was not easy at all. By the grace of God, I graduated with honors.

Shortly after graduating from Bible School, I interviewed for an administrative position with my church and was hired to work full-time. So, there I was working as one of the admins for the Dean of the Bible School. For a moment, I felt I had settled into what had become my life's calling – "working for the church". However, the Lord had bigger plans for me. Look at what Isaiah 55:8-9 has to say.

> *"For my thoughts are not your thoughts, nor are your ways my ways, says the Lord. For as the heavens are higher than the earth; So are*

my ways higher than your ways, and my thoughts than your thoughts."

The blessings and plans God has for our lives are beyond anything we can fathom.

Reality Shock

I got comfortable in my administrative position with the church until an announcement was made that changes were taken place amongst the staff. I was reassigned to the Accounting Department. At first, I was upset, but I had to chill and be grateful that I still had a job and my pay was not cut. Not to mention, the ministry is not going to put just anyone around the finances. During a quiet moment in the office, the ladies started talking about purpose and knowing if you were really in God's will or not for your life. One of the ladies looked at me said to the effect, "Addie, I know this is not what you expected. You were used to be being around a group that is more "elite." However, I believe God ordained your steps to be with us. As you move on, you are going to be around people from all walks of life. You need to be able to converse and relate to them." As I look back over that moment in my life, my former co-worker hit the nail on the head.

I think about the many times of stepping out into the unknown with big ambitions. However, the problem is that I did not fully consider the pros and cons of my "acts of faith." As I mentioned a little earlier in our reading, I moved away from Detroit, Michigan, and attempted to establish myself in Jackson, Mississippi. After only working in the ministry there for nearly seven months, I ended up being laid off. I thought to myself, "Now what in the heck is going on? God, I need answers?" Not to mention, life ended up being a little bit tougher than expected. I thought I had all my ducks in a row. However, I did not consider the unexpected. I was walking by faith and learning many lessons along the way. As I mentioned earlier in this chapter, God's plan for me was much bigger. I was not called to permanently work in full-time church ministry. I was only in that arena to learn. Other situations transpired that were either a lesson or a blessing, if not both.

So, here I was back in the corporate world. To some, this return would seem like a failure. But, the disappointment of failed ambitions and dreams only served to be redirection. I had to learn to separate reality from fantasy and fact from fiction. I had to let go of the fantasy and fiction of love, ministry, and life in general. It was a tough wakeup call for me. My return to the corporate world was a call to be light and bring ministry to those who needed it most. After facing an abrupt end to church ministry, I soon launched two online devotionals called "Midnight Oil" and "Healing Oil." I even created a website called Healing Oil Ministries. Sharing words of life and encouragement not only helped others, but it helped me to heal and grow stronger. There was no ceiling in ministry for me. I found myself being equipped in ways that Bible School and my college degree did not teach me.

More Equipped

As an author and encourager, I am not into coming for people or acting like I have all the answers. By sharing my story, the goal is to share some light and nuggets of wisdom to help someone else. I might have already mentioned what I am about to say, but this is not my first time putting a formal book together. Writing a book and other endeavors do not happen overnight. It is a process. I look back over the years of trying different things to get ahead. I would even fall in and out of love with men during my single season until I decided to let go, breathe, and let God lead the way. My character had to be shaped and developed. I also had to go through a refining process. There was more I had to learn and experience in my life so my story could be richer and purposeful.

When you complete an application for a job and turn in a resume, you are asked about your work experience. After you make it to the actual interview, you are asked how you handled certain situations. Those experiences, along with whatever training you received, help you to be more marketable and equipped. However, there is something greater than experience. It is wisdom. I have gray hair that I dye to maintain a sassy and sophisticated look. However, the gray can be stubborn, insisting on letting everyone know it has the right to be here (smile). Some people would say that gray hair is a sign of wisdom, but not necessarily. You can be older but not wiser. Wisdom in and of itself is one of the greatest tools and treasures you can have. The Book of Proverbs talks about the value and essence of having wisdom. It is wisdom that makes us more equipped to make better decisions and provide counsel to others.

Wisdom accompanied by discernment has empow-ered me. I was taught to walk by faith. However, faith without wisdom and discernment can lead to a messy life. I do not regret walking by faith and following the Holy Spirit, because what is born out of true faith will prosper. Some things I went through were part of my process. On the other hand, there were things I did not have to go through. There were so many lessons learned. These lessons became blessings and made me a better woman overall.

Lessons Learned

There are so many lessons I have learned up to this point and time in my life. Let's be real. Life is constantly schooling you. If you have eyes to see and ears to hear, there is always something new to learn. One thing I have learned that is life is not an arrival; it is a journey. You never get to the place where you know everything. It does not matter if you are an expert in your field and gifted, you are always a student of life. God sets before you another opportunity to grow. This brings me to another lesson. I have learned to not be too comfortable with being comfortable. Yes, you want to feel comfortable in a home, car, outfit, a pair of glasses, etc. However, I am referring to staying in a place of growth. Growing is a good thing, but it is not always easy. It is a process that says- "This will not happen overnight. But, if you walk this out, the results will be amazing."

Another important lesson I want to share with you is the significance of open and closed doors. When God opens a door, His favor and grace will go before you. His spirit is there to guide you through every step. However, you must have the courage to put one foot in front of the other and move forward. When a door is closed, I have learned that it could be protection and/or redirection. I remember applying for a certain job when I lived in Detroit. I was so excited about the potential pay and hours being presented to me. I was devasted when I found out the job had been offered to someone else. Upon giving the situation some thought, I realized that God was protecting me from something I could not see. He was also redirecting me towards something better.

I want to share another vital lesson involving self-care. This includes, spiritually, mentally, and physically. During my early years of serving in church ministries, I was taught to put God first and to serve others. Yes, indeed, God comes first in terms of our relationship with Him along with keeping your faith strong. However, the next person in line is you. I say this because loving your neighbor as yourself does not mean to neglect yourself. There was a season in my life that was very rough. I spent so much time making sure others were okay, that I neglected my health and well-being. Stress and worry caused me to drop down from a size 10 to a size 4. I was losing too much weight as I allowed depression to set in. Upon removing myself from what was toxic, I felt like I could breathe and live again. I learned that it is okay to put the oxygen mask on yourself first then you can help others.

As I close out this segment, I want you to know that waterfalls are beautiful. I saw one up close and personal when my father took the family to Niagara Falls many years ago. However, the beautiful cascade of water does not have the power to sustain you. Waterfalls are unstable and do not have a solid foundation for anyone to stand upon. I have learned to enjoy the beauty of a waterfall, but I must not chase them. I look to God who gives me hinds feet (see Habakkuk 3:19) to walk and stand in the place of purpose and divine destiny that is my calling.

Chapter 6:
God's Plan

"Many plans are in a man's mind, but it is the Lord's purpose for him that will stand."

-Proverbs 19:21

You Can't Go Back!

During the early part of 2006, I had a dream that left a lasting impact on me. I awaken from my sleep in the earlier morning hours and noticed a bright light shining from my master bathroom door. (Technically, I was still sleeping). I sat up in the bed with curiosity. As I began to approach the door to investigate, a woman appeared dressed in white, who resembled someone from my early childhood days in the church. She was guarding the door and pointing me away from it. It was at this point that I woke up. This dream stayed heavily on my mind. When I returned to work, I mentioned the dream to a guy named Robert. He was very focused on his work. At the same time, he was not secretive about his faith in God and Pentecostal roots. I decided to share my dream with Robert because I knew him to be very discerning about certain things.

After describing the dream in detail, Robert stating that my dream had significance, but he was unable to help me with any interpretation. However, as Robert began to walk away from my desk, he suddenly stopped, turned around, and walked back towards me. He said- "Your dream means to remember where you come from, thank God for what He has brought you through, but you can't go back!" Also, the angelic lady in my dream represented the past and the closed-door was for redirection. So, there I was with the words engraved in my spirit "You can't go back!" This did not mean that I could not go back to my hometown of Detroit to visit.

However, I was not to return to a lifestyle of familiarity. The Lord wanted to do something new in my life. Even though I had received these words at the time, it took me a little while to truly embrace the process of moving forward and trusting God to do a new thing.

When I think about it, I had moved physically from state to state, from one apartment to the next, but there was a shift that had to take place in my mind. Moving forward requires renewing your mind because you will go no further than the mindset that you have. In the Bible, Romans 12:2 talks about renewing your mind. It does not say that God is going to do it. You must do the work. In my dream/vision, I was admonished not to go back. What is it that God is telling you to move on from? For me, it was tradition and religion. I want to be clear in saying that not all traditions are bad. I am just referring to tradition and religion that keeps you stagnate or going in circles. Well, as I said earlier, it took me a moment to embrace the process of moving in a new direction. I kept going around the same mountain because I wanted to hold on to what was familiar.

Losing My Way

I was raised in the church. I came to know the Lord as a teenager. My parents signed me up to be part of a youth ministry. As mentioned earlier in this book, after becoming a young adult, I chose a church ministry to be a part of and stayed with that fellowship for several years. Outside of the church and away from the saints, I watched my favorite TV shows, listened to a variety of music, read mystery books, and epic novels, played board games, studied, and worked part-time. Oh, let me not forget to mention that I read my Bible most days. A lady that I met in college blessed me with a Living Bible from the bookstore she worked at inside of Northland Mall in Michigan. This mall is now closed permanently, but I cherish the season of friendship that brought this valuable possession into my life. This precious Bible is still in my life. Through my ups and downs, peaks, and valleys, this Living Bible has been a constant companion.

I was in a season of being on my way to becoming something great. It was the late 80s, and this young adult felt like she had her footing on solid ground. However, life has a way of exposing what most people cannot see. I was still plagued with brokenness, insecurities, and the need to be genuinely loved and accepted. As a result, I struggled with self-harm, fell in and out of love, and was occasionally haunted by issues and mistakes I wished was not a part of my story. However, God has a way of taking what we regret and making something beautiful out of it. While there are some things we do not have to go through, we all need a little dirt to grow along with sunshine and rain. Again, it is not my endeavor to stand before anyone perfect, as I am far from it. When I think about the times that I lost my way, our Heavenly Father was right there saying, "I love you. I have not given up on you. I've got you! Do not give up on yourself!"

When we lose our way and life does not go as planned, I am reminded of a passage in the Bible that says the following:

"For My thoughts are not your thoughts, nor are your ways my ways," says the LORD. For as the heavens are higher than the earth, so are My ways

higher than your ways, and My thoughts than your thoughts." (Isaiah 55:8-9)

God's ways and thoughts are not just higher, they are perfect. If you are like me, there may be do-overs you would like to have. However, when I look at my life now, I thank God for keeping me and for having a love that never fails and never gives up on me. I also thank myself for not quitting or giving up. If you could have a conversation with the younger version of yourself, what you way say to him or her? If I could go back and chat with my younger self, I would assure her to not fret or worry and to trust and never doubt.

Restored

To be candid, I have lost my way on several occasions. I was a child of God who did not realize I was free to live an abundant life. The prison doors to my soul were open by the love, mercy, and grace of God, but I went through a phase of running back into bondage. I thank God for not giving up on me and for helping me not give up on myself. I am grateful for new beginnings and restoration. Webster's Dictionary uses the following words to describe "restore": to bring back, reinstate, replace, rehabilitate, repair, and return. I had to go through a spiritual car wash of being cleaned up and polished with each described application of the word "restore." Just like an automobile needs to be washed and detailed, so do our spirit and souls. This cleansing is not always due to falling by the wayside. Sometimes a good cleansing is needed to refresh us from being overwhelmed by the challenges of life. I love the following Scripture in Matthew 11:28-30 (The Message Bible), has to say.

"Are you tired? Worn out? Burned out on religion? Come to me. Get away with me and you'll recover your life. I'll show you how to take a real rest. Walk with me and work with me—watch how I do it. Learn the unforced rhythms of grace. I won't lay anything heavy or ill-fitting on you. Keep company with me and you'll learn to live freely and lightly."

Now, I will say, "Yes and Amen" on that one! My soul needed to be set free from ungodly soul ties, toxic relationships, people-pleasing, religion, negative words that taunted me, opinions, the guilt of bad decisions, fear, worry, and insecurities. Even to this very moment, I work to guard my heart and keep my mind free of things that come to agitate my peace and joy. We are given peace and joy that the world did not give and cannot take away.

The Grace of God has kept me when I did not want to be kept. Can anyone reading relate to this? You may be asking, "Now, why would she not want God to keep her?" There were times I just wanted what I wanted even if it was bad for me. This state of mind causes a person to undervalue themselves. I am so glad to have remained a member of a royal priesthood in God's eyes even though I was not acting like it. I briefly think about how I lost everything in terms of material things along with dignity, but the Lord has restored me and my family to overflowing. If I sound like I am giving testimony and having a brief praise break, I am! To live in restoration and experience new beginnings is priceless. If you are not where you want or need to be, it is my prayer for you to healed, restored, and made whole. May you walk in the fullness of all that you were designed for by God.

Lessons Learned, Part 2

I shared about lessons learned in the previous chapter. But, in this segment, I want to speak on seeing failure and losses from a different perspective. Look at the quote I have documented at the beginning of this chapter. It says, "Sometimes you win, and sometimes you learn." When I first heard that quote, it caused me to slow down, pause, and think about it for a moment. Remember that failure is not final. If you have lived to overcome and tell the story, was the situation failure or a lesson learned? Also, if you experienced a loss or setback, what did you learn? What was the takeaway from the experience?

In November of 2014, I took the time to visit with my Mom in Detroit, who became extremely ill from heart complications. At that time, I did not realize it would be my last time seeing her. She passed away after suffering from two strokes. After her passing, I reflected on lessons to be learned. I thought about the importance of forgiveness, letting go and letting God, what mattered in life, along with a bunch of other thoughts. After my family laid my mother to rest, I meditated on lessons becoming blessings. This does not mean that everything you experience in life is a blessing. However, the lessons learned make you better, stronger, and wiser. What was meant to turn you bitter makes you better.

As it is written in Romans 8:28, "And we know that all things work together for good to those who love God, to those who are the called according to *His* purpose."

The Scripture I just shared is often misquoted or taken out of context. People quote the first part of the verse and leave out the second part. It is important to consider the whole of the Scripture and realize that God has a way of taking situations that did not go well or meant for harm and cause them to align with his purpose for our lives. Our pain can transition into purpose. So, again there is a lesson in every situation because it works out for our good. We are students of life as we go from one level of destiny to the next.

CHAPTER 7:
TO BE REAL

"The more you like yourself, the less you are like anyone else, which makes you unique."

-Walt Disney

This chapter will be an extension of the chapter entitled "Musical Identity." So much of what we do or do not do hinges on who we have become, whether genuine or fake. In this millennial age, we are amongst a generation that has developed a low tolerance for what is fake. When video blogs and TV shows highlight real aspects of a person's life, the viewers find it welcoming and entertaining. While I am personally not a fan of reality TV that is scripted and dramatized, I understand the appetite needed for this type of viewing. People want what is real. In this segment, we will peel back those layers that have hidden or buried who we are. It is time for the "real" you to stand up strong and fearless!

Everyone Else Taken

I once saw a quote on social media that says, "Be yourself, everyone else is taken." I do not know who the originator of the quote is, but it speaks volumes. Trying to be like somebody else is like trying to fit into an outfit that is tailored made for another person. Your life will not fit into a script that is designed for someone else. There is no "one size fits all" when it comes to being who we are designed to be. The struggle is real "to be real" when you are taunted by a past full of secrets, hurt, pain, rejection, abuse, and failure. The things that taunt you make you feel like you can never get over them. As mentioned in previous chapters, I had to get over being called "slow," bullied, rejected, and disappointed. I had to get over feeling like a failure in situations that did not work out. Negative life experiences can beat you down and make you feel ashamed. You end up hiding the real you underneath a wardrobe of layers.

Speaking of layers, an onion has layers. Like an onion is uncovered, peeled back, and prepared to add spice and flavor to a meal, so it is with you and me. As a child of God, you were meant to add spice and flavor to life. However, this cannot happen if we are stacked behind a bunch of layers. I remember being in a religious meeting where a woman of God was teaching on spiritual gifts and using them to help others. She sensed that many of us in the room were holding back due to insecurities or walls we had put up. She mentioned that our spirits and souls needed to be peeled back like an onion. Hiding beneath all the layers is the one and only you.

I want you to realize there is no one like you on the planet. You are a designer original. One major thing that makes each one of us original is our finger and footprints. Unless something is done to alter those prints, our finger and footprints are not the same. This is amazing in and of itself. Please review and meditate for a few seconds on the quote at the top of this chapter. So many people struggle with identity because they do not like themselves. Not liking yourself is self-hatred. It is saying, "I wish I was not me. I wish I could be somebody else!" This self-hatred can come from circumstances beyond our control or bad decisions made while trying to find your way.

What you have gone through is not who you are. It is only "What you have gone through." When the dust settles from the drama and the storm calms down, who are you? If you are struggling with identity, look at yourself in the mirror and say, "I am God's chosen. He loves me. I love myself. I am beautiful. I am amazing. I am intelligent. I am smart. I am kind. I am beautiful. I am handsome. I am light. I am unique. I have a bright future. I have flavor. I add spice to life." The list can go on and on. I took myself through this exercise when I engaged in a 90-Day coaching program before writing this book. Trust me when I tell you that the positive use of words to describe and highlight yourself will uplift you. When you speak life over yourself, it is like charging a car battery. You will be able to go the extra mile.

Face to Face

Right here, we will confront anything from within or without that is keeping you from being your genuine and authentic self. Several years ago, I quoted, "You cannot defeat giants you will not confront." There is a well-known Bible Story about David and Goliath (please see I Samuel 17). I know that many of you heard of it. This Philistine Giant taunts and mocks the King of Israel (Saul) and the people. An average guy named David (soon to be King of Israel) offers to confront the giant. He does so with the grace and strength given to him by God. David swings a rock in a sling and slays the giant in the forehead. I used this story to parallel the personal giants that keep us from loving ourselves and being all that we are meant to be. I want to go deeper on this point with a personal situation that took place during my childhood.

From the age of 5 years old to 9 years old, I repeatedly dreamed of a werewolf woman. It did not happen every night, but on most nights it did. I was terrified to go to sleep because of this continuous nightmare. I remember telling my father that something was bothering me. Sometimes, my dad would sit up with me and pray until I was sound asleep. After I turned 9 years old, the evil presence showed up in my sleep, this time I had enough. I heard a voice speak to me and say, "Tell it to leave you alone!" I clenched my fists, looked at the werewolf woman, and said, "Leave me alone!!" I woke up and never had a dream like that again. I did not have a relationship with God like that I do now, but I knew the Lord was with me. I believe that one of God's angels (a messenger) whispered into my subconscious ear to tell me how to fight back. I hope this example helps you to confront your giant, whether it be a demon, fear, insecurity, lack, disease, opinions, and so forth.

Before we move forward, I want to mention the number one person I have found to keep me stuck is the woman I look at in the mirror every day. The biggest enemy of my destiny is me. Things happened that were not my fault. Some things cannot be changed, but I have to ask myself, "What can I change? How can I help myself?" I praise God for how I have grown and overcome so many hurdles and obstacles. Regularly, I pray and work at maintaining a sound mind, and encouraging myself when I feel down. It is not about being perfect, but it is about remaining in a constant state of improvement.

Loving You

As I share my heart and nuggets of wisdom with you, I think about the word "love." I have a decorative piece in my master bathroom that says, "Love never fails." This comes from I Corinthians 13 in the Bible. Love is a pure and powerful word that has been abused and misused over the centuries of mankind's existence on this planet. I will be honest in telling you that for a season in my life, I was immature and naïve to "real love." I once had relationships in my life that were based on circumstances and everything going their way. Like many children of God, I knew that God loved me, but I had to learn to love myself. I am not talking about being vain, conceited, or self-righteous. When the Bible talks about love being patient, kind, longsuffering, believing the best, and not being rude that agape love should begin with you. The way you see yourself determines how you will respond to situations along with what you give and accept.

I have a friend from Detroit, Michigan, who I am also friends with on Facebook who quoted, "Love your neighbor as yourself, not despite yourself." Of course, I had to give that post a thumbs up. Loving others and giving to everyone else is a noble thing. However, this should never happen at the expense of maintaining your spiritual, mental, and physical well-being. During the summer of 2018, I was at work moving from one office to a new one. I suddenly began to feel ill. My heart rate and blood pressure began to spike. I was blessed to be amongst a group of colleagues, who were trained EMTs and First Responders. One of them had to restart my heart. I was stabilized and rushed to Emory Medical Hospital in Decatur, Georgia. The medical team was top notch. My husband was on the road and felt helpless because he was not there, but God was there. Two colleagues stayed with me and several people checked on me. I was blessed to walk out of the hospital like nothing ever happened.

There was a lesson to be learned from this experience that I shared with you. I needed to take better care of myself from the inside-out. I also learned not to take on more than I should. It is okay to say, "no" when you need to say it. It is also important to make time to rest, relax, and have fun. The world will not fall apart because you take a break. It is not selfish to go bowling with close friends, go for a walk, watch a good movie, get a mani-pedi, take a vacation, or just do nothing. You do not always have to be doing the most. The better you are to yourself, the better you will be for others.

Before I close out this piece of our discussion, I want you to know that "loving you" means to apply the principles of Agape Love to yourself (Read I Corinthians 13). Be patient with yourself. If you are trying to improve your health and fitness, know that it will take time to get in shape and see the results that you want. Be longsuffering with yourself. Sometimes, we can be our hardest critics. Yes, you should challenge yourself to be better. However, take some of the pressure off yourself, and do not be so quick to give up when things don't go as planned. Be kind to yourself. It is so important to be your own best friend. Speak life over yourself and believe the best about yourself. Train yourself to think better about yourself. Work to eliminate self-hatred. See yourself the way God sees you.

Being You

Earlier in this chapter, I made mention of fingerprints and footprints. No one on the planet has the same prints. This means you were meant to be a designer original. You were meant to be uniquely you. Some situations may have been difficult, and people may have said some crazy stuff to you over the years, but those negative experiences do not stop who you are truly meant to be. Situations happen that we did not choose, but God's plan for your life still stands. Know that God chose you! The enemy of our souls works overtime to keep us from knowing who we truly are and living a life of purpose. When you are rooted in God and aware of who you were meant to be, this causes havoc on the kingdom of darkness. Knowing who you are, you will bring light and life to your pathway. When you awaken to the beauty of life originally given to you, there is a God-confidence that cannot be shaken. As is says in Proverbs 3:26, "For the Lord will be your confidence, he will keep your foot from being trapped."

Let us talk a little bit about flaws or imperfections. When I was a young girl, I remember being eleven years old with a size 10 shoe. I also had to start wearing glasses, and I inherited a gap in my front teeth from my mother. I was not fond of my shoe size at all. I felt my genetics failed to consult with me on the ideal height, weight, and physical features I desired to have. I was teased about my shoe size, and I was called "Frankenstein feet." I laugh at that now, but back in the day, this was not funny to me. The thing is that I did not realize I was beautiful. Yes, I was in an awkward stage in my development, but I was beautiful. I was blossoming into the young lady I was designed to be. As I grew into adulthood, I accepted my size ten shoes and found beautiful shoes to adorn my feet with. I was no longer self-conscious about wearing glasses as I was surrounded by several people who wore them. When it came to my teeth, I eventually had surgery and wore braces for 18 months. I enhanced my physical features, but, again, I was beautiful because God said so!

The beauty, handsomeness, and sexiness we seek begin from within. We may have eyes of different colors, scars, beauty marks, big feet, tiny feet, vary in height and weight, and the list goes on and on. However, I believe every flaw or imperfection serves a purpose in developing and shaping our stories. When I was a child, running around in my parent's backyard, I remember stumbling over a few rocks and falling. With tears in my eyes, I grabbed my right knee. My mom placed ointment on my little wound and put a bandage on it. As wounds begin to heal, your original color of flesh begins to restore itself. However, in some cases like mine, you are left with a scar. I grew up with this scar reminding me of when I fell on those rocks. Guess what? The scar has faded, but it is still there. I am not ashamed of the scar because it reminds me, that although I fell, I got back up. Allow your scars to serve as a victory badge of what you survived and lived to tell the story of. Being you involves allowing your imperfections and beauty marks to signify what makes you special and unique.

As we bring this chapter to a close, I want you to meditate on what sets you apart from anyone else. Think about the talent, ability, or special gift you have. How can you use one of those attributes to help you shine and be a blessing to others? You and I were meant to be more than just the next average person going through the motions of life. Realizing that you are one of a kind is the essence of being you. I encourage you to celebrate what makes you special and unique. Do not compare yourself to anyone else. Let go of the fears and insecurities that have held you back. Decide to be true to who you are. Realize that you are perfect for your purpose. Be real and live abundantly!

CHAPTER 8:
YOUR LIFE MATTERS

"You meant for me to soar. I am your child. And, I'm worth fighting for."

-Brian Courtney Wilson

Who Told You That??

I am going to get straight to the point on this one. Anything that does not line up with what God says about you, and anything not spoken out of love is a lie! When you are subjected to circumstances out of your control or do not know your worth, the lie can seem like the truth. We are going to dismantle those lies with the truth. I love what it says in John 8:32, "You shall know the truth, and the truth shall make you free." The truth will set you free not keep you in bondage. When the truth comes in the form of constructive criticism, it may cut, but it will quickly restore and build you back up. It will set you free. I used to live under so many lies that had to be dismantled. This dismantling was done through prayer, the Holy Spirit, and renewing my mind with the right things. I had to train myself to say and become the opposite of what was spoken about me. I had to stop saying crazy things about myself. I want to put the following lies on blast that have been told to many people:

- "You are never going to amount to anything!" Who told you that?? So many people have been told that lie by a family member, schoolteacher, so-called friend, or a religious person. Even if your life was or is headed in the wrong direction, this is not true. No one has the right to make that proclamation over your life. A touch from God, an awakening, and the courage to fight can turn your life in the right direction.

- "You will never be good enough." Who told you that?? In addition to other people telling you this, what makes it worse is when we say something like this to ourselves. Failure and not being the brightest or most talented at something does not make this statement true. There will always be someone, who is better at something or has more than you. Do not compare yourself to others. Find what you are good at. Develop the gift, talent, or ability that you possess. If something in your life needs to change for the better, take the steps necessary to make the change. Be grateful for what you have. Learn to love you and the skin you are in.

- "You aren't worth two cents!" Who told you that?? People will say this to someone in a joking or sarcastic manner. You or someone you know may have laughed this off, but the statement is negative. No one has the right to discount you. It is also important not to discount yourself to make other people feel comfortable with you. The right people will celebrate you, not tolerate you.

Our words have power. Proverbs 18:21 says, "Life and death are in the power of the tongue." Before I met my husband, I had to shake myself out of the dark hole I fell into. I knew that I wanted real love in my life, but I was afraid of falling into another place of heartbreak and disappointment. So, I kept saying, "I do not trust myself." I was speaking out of fear and insecurity. One day, I heard the Lord speak to my heart, "Why do you keep saying that? If you want your prayers answered, stop saying that!" I not only had to trust God, but I also had to trust in my ability to love again. I had to renew my mind and place my heart in God's hand to receive the real love that was waiting for me. I decided to speak life moving forward. What other people believe or say about you is one thing, but you believe and speak over your own life can make or break you. People are entitled to their opinions, but if they are not speaking from a place of wisdom, take their words with a grain of salt. Speak life and meditate on what is true, lovely, honest, and of a good report (see Philippians 4:8).

Worth Fighting For

Pause, go to the internet on your phone or computer, and pull up the song entitled "Worth Fighting For" by Brian Courtney Wilson. That song is so inspiring and enco-uraging. I want to ask you something. What are you currently fighting for? I briefly think about things I once felt were worth fighting for. As a train of thought, when it comes to fighting, we must choose our battles wisely. The outcome of what we fight for will either be a win, a lesson, or a loss altogether. In my past life, I remember fighting to keep a man in my life. That man did not want me the way I wanted him. There was absolutely nothing I could do or say to make him stay in my life. He needed to walk in his truth and keep it moving. I was left in my pride and embarrassment of trying to make someone love me. I was fighting for fantasy and not for what represented true purpose and value. Can anyone relate to that?

What is worth fighting for are the following: your life, your spiritual well-being, your mind, your health, your marriage, your family, your purpose, or a solid dream and vision. One of the major things I had to fight for is mental wellness. I have seen the toll that mental illness has had on my life. I am not ashamed to talk about it, because it is about helping other people get the help they need and be set free. I will never forget the day my dad looked at me and said, "Mental illness runs in the family. Guard your heart and mind." I looked at him and thought to myself, "Thanks for the info, but I rebuke that in Jesus' name!" However, my dad knew that he needed help and wanted to forewarn me of the dangers and challenges that come with denying that a problem exists. I found myself confronting my demons and engaging in a battlefield for my peace and sanity. I spent many nights praying, standing on God's Word, and keeping my surroundings positive. I thank God for keeping me in my right mind. I thank God for strengthening my Dad and other people I know and love.

Many of you reading this have some stories to share things you have fought for. Some of you may be going through some current challenges right now. If that is the case, do not be ashamed of what you have been through or are currently going through. Psalm 23:4 says, "Yea, though I walk through the valley of the shadow of death, I will fear no evil...." The keyword is "through." Webster's Dictionary defines "through" as moving on one side and stepping out on the other side. Wow! Let that definition sink in your spirit for a moment. Whatever life challenges us with, we have more grace and strength than we realize to go through (to go in one way and come out the other way). You do not have to waddle in hurt, pain, despair, loneliness, grief, and so on. Yes, these things are real to the human experience. There were times when I did not see how I was going to make it, but now I look back and see that I made it through. I came out on the other side. One year during Thanksgiving, my son said- "I am thankful because every time it looked like there was no way, God made a way."

If you are reading this and feel like giving up, please do not! Things may look worse now, people may be judging you, but the storm will pass. It is so important to have an anchor. An anchor keeps a ship or boat from drifting off into the sea. What is your anchor? What is holding you up? That thing cannot be a quick fix. There are things you cannot drink away, smoke away, sleep away, medicate away, or sex away. It must be something solid like your faith, hope, friendship, love, and a word that uplifts you. When challenges come, and they will, do not lose heart. Stand in faith and fight for what God has promised you! Fight for your dreams and visions. Fight for what you know is worth fighting for. Be steadfast, unmovable, and living by faith. Your life is worth fighting for.

Your Story, God's Glory

It is my prayer that many hearts will be blessed, inspired, and encouraged through the words written in this book thus far. For some of you, life is good. For some, life is good, but it could be better. For others reading this book, life is very challenging. One thing is certain, life is truly an experience of highs and lows along with sunshine and rain. Everyone reading this book is loved by God. You are special and here for a purpose. Your journey and your story are your highlight reel. Do not be ashamed of what you have been through. You are an awesome being birthed into this world for such a time as this. You are a seed planted by God to develop a life that springs up like a tree and producing healthy fruit. Allow your spirit to receive the right amount of soil, water, and sunshine so you can grow.

I encourage you as I encourage myself that nothing you have gone through was a waste. Yes, maybe somethings could have been done better. Maybe, you could have made better decisions in certain chapters of your life. There may even be scenes you wish never took place at all. However, I want you to remember what is written in Romans 8:28 that says, "All things work together for the good of those, who love God and are called according to his purpose." God can take what was meant for evil and turn it around to give power and purpose to your story. I thank God for keeping me and bringing me through moments of helplessness, darkness, hurt, betrayal, loss, rejection, shame, mistakes, and bad decisions. I am grateful for so many opportunities to begin again and to become a better woman and human being.

You and I are here today by the Grace of God. If your eyes are reading the pages of this book and you are on this page, it is because God is still writing your story. There is more to do and accomplish. Someone needs what God has placed on the inside of you to give them life, hope, and encouragement. Someone needs to be able to look at your life and say. If they can do it, I can too! I celebrate your successes and pray for you to overcome any obstacle you are currently facing. Live each day with purpose. In this fast-paced world, we can miss out on the simple beauty of life given to us. I encourage you to slow down a little and take in the blue skies, sunshine, flowers, the smile of a child, the smell of freshly brewed coffee, and the warm embrace of someone who loves you.

Your life matters. Your story is for God's glory. Join me for one more chapter in this book as I share brief highlights of my journey past and present. I will give you a sneak peek of what is to come as well. It is my highlight reel, my truth. I am grateful for this moment and the time we have had together. I bid you shalom- peace, nothing missing, and nothing broken.

Chapter 9:
SINCERELY YOURS

"Don't be ashamed of your past. Your story and what God has brought you through could be the very thing that helps someone else have the courage to keep trying!"

–Angie Gray

In the Beginning

My beginning took place in Detroit, Michigan. I was named Addie by my parents Clyde and Vivian. Addie means "noble," and I was named after my great-grandmother Addie Beatrice Smith. She was my father's grandmother from Sweetwater, Tennessee, and he was very fond of her. I am the eldest of three girls. I am blessed to have my sister Lorita still in my life as our third sister Christa has passed away along with my mother Vivian. Growing up in Detroit was a good life overall. However, my life in Detroit was not without its growing pains, peaks and valleys, joy, and tears. At an early age, I struggled in elementary and part of middle school. Despite my learning disability, I had become an avid reader. I remember the joy I felt when my mother would order books from Scholastic Books. Sometimes my Dad would take us to the main Detroit Public Library, which still stands today in the cultural district of the city. I would sit up late at night reading a good book. Reading was educational, personal medicine, and an escape from reality.

One of the best times of my life was spent with my mother's side of the family. The family picnics, short trips to places like Cedar Point in Sandusky, Ohio, Christmas Eve at my Aunt Henrietta's house, and Christmas at my Grandma Maggie's house were the best! As mentioned earlier in this book, I dealt with bullying in elementary and part of middle school.

Things got better for me socially and academically in the eighth grade. I attended Murray-Wright High School. I made the honor roll consistently and enjoyed my four years there. After graduation from high school and then college, I thought I was ready for the world. However, life had some lessons for me that you cannot find in a syllabus, textbook, or classroom lecture. There were things I had to walk through and learn the lesson that came with the experience. I fell in and out of love a few times, got married, had two children, and ended up divorced. I, along with my two babies, temporarily moved back in with my parents and started life over again.

I thank God for all the opportunities given to me to become a better woman. After I separated from my first husband, I began to journal almost every day. Writing what was on my heart, along with jotting down dreams and goals, provided a healing element in my life. I was so hurt and angry after my divorce. Journaling helped to restore life and hope to me. I was not one of those people who only wrote about complaints. I wrote about praise reports, things I was thankful for and lessons learned. While I am on this train of thought, I encourage you to purchase a journal to write down your thoughts. Be honest about where you are and where you need to be. Journaling will keep you from sinking in despair. It will help you to overcome fear, worry, depression, and anxiety. As time went on, I began to write devotions to share over the internet with others. I started with AOL. Remember the saying, "You've got mail!" Like the Bible says, "Do not despise small beginnings."

I knew for many years I wanted to write and publish books to bless and encourage others. However, I was still a work in progress. I had to slay a few giants and confront the demons that kept taunting me. Life tested and challenged me like it does anyone else. As this book is called Highlight Reel, I had to get to the place of becoming genuine and authentic in sharing my story and the wisdom I have gained. Living a life that is genuine, blessed, and fearless begins with being true to yourself. You must face fear, guilt, shame, addiction, insecurity, and whatever is causing you to lack in areas of your life head-on. Always remember that you cannot slay giants you do not confront. Whatever your beginning might have been, good or bad, you are here at this moment in time because your story is not over.

Present Day

At this very moment, I am sitting in my home at my desk with a small lamp on. It is a Sunday evening in Georgia. I sit looking out the front window of my home as the sun begins to set. The day has been beautiful and full of sunshine. My husband-Michael and nephew-Gabriel are relaxing in our family room with a good movie. Our son and daughter are in their rooms studying. The school year is ending through online learning. Bryan is graduating from college and Kayla is graduating from high school. We have an older daughter -Tiara who is out on her own, currently teaching English to elementary school kids. Our pet-Starr is having a fit for attention. She is spoiled, and it is our fault (smile). My home and family are intact and favored by the Grace of God. Yet, the world around us is faced with unprecedented circumstances.

A global Pandemic shifted one reality we were living in into another. Government leaders encouraged their citizens to curb their normal activities and shelter in place to curb the spread of a virus, which I will not name. Many people have been blessed to overcome and dodge the bullet of the virus. One person blessed to heal and recover from the virus is one of my close cousins, name Tony in my hometown of Detroit along with his son. Also, a high school classmate beat the virus as well. Praise God! However, some have not been so fortunate. Much prayer has been needed to stay in faith and be positive despite this reality. It feels like we have been living in a *Twilight Zone*, but I can personally say that God has kept and provided for us through it all.

This segment of writing to you was not originally planned, but it is no accident as some things happen the way it is supposed to happen. At this moment, I work from home and homeschool my nephew. That part, the homeschool thing has been a challenge, to say the least. However, I realize that I am equipped for the task. Prayer, Google, and a good working relationship with Gabriel's teachers have gotten us through. Zoom has been the thing for work, ministry, and social meetings as "social distancing" is the standard until a healthier climate comes into view. I have to say that I have been grateful for a slower pace. There has been more time to think, quality time with family, and the ability to complete this book. More is to come as this is only the beginning of other books and endeavors. Greater is coming!

To Be Continued....

Typically, a "comma" represents a pause or break in a sentence. It also signifies the continuation of a sentence. Whereas a "period" represents the end of a sentence. Sometimes life and some people will look at you and place a period where God has a comma. As I mentioned earlier, I thank God for the opportunities He has given me to begin again and become a better woman. I say that because there were times when I doubted my ability to be a shining light and make a difference in this world. I had to awaken to who I was meant to be and take my power back. Yes, I made mistakes. There are things I could have done better. However, my situations were not the end of my life. If you are at a place of feeling like you lack purpose, direction, or significance, I want to encourage you to not give up on yourself. Do not place a period where God has a comma. Your story is to be continued. It is not too late to be all you can be and become the best version of yourself.

If your highlight reel is not allowing you to live a life that is genuine, blessed, and fearless, then it is time to change some things. Take off the masks that are hiding the real you. If you are in a career that is not complimenting you, now is the time to make the change. If you need to go back to school, go! If you desire to start a non-profit or business, do your research, utilize resources, and get started. Do not become someone you are not to fit in. You do yourself and others a disservice when you are being someone you are not, do not compare yourself to another person's highlight reel on social media. Always remember that people share what they choose and keep other things private. You never truly know what is going on behind a smile and a nice pose.

If you think you are too old to accomplish certain dreams and goals, it is not too late if you have the mind, health, and strength to do it. Your life is not a period but a comma because God is still writing your story! Your story is for God's glory. Thank you again for being on this journey with me. I look forward to sharing with you again in books to follow and other platforms. Be blessed, and live a life that is genuine, blessed, and fearless!

Sincerely yours,

Addie Lee Hention

ABOUT THE AUTHOR

Addie Lee Hention is a native of Detroit, Michigan. She is a graduate of Davenport University, formerly Detroit College of Busines, with a B.A. in Business Administration. Addie has written several blogs, and she had two devotionals entitled Midnight Oil and Healing Oil. She had an internet Blog Talk Radio show that ran from 2010-2012. She has also been a guest speaker on other internet radio shows and conference calls. Addie has used her social media platform to inspire, motive and encourage many people. Addie currently resides in Georgia with her husband Michael and their blended family. Together they have one teenager and five adult children.

www.ingramcontent.com/pod-product-compliance
Lightning Source LLC
Chambersburg PA
CBHW070953080526
44587CB00015B/2291

9781734060966